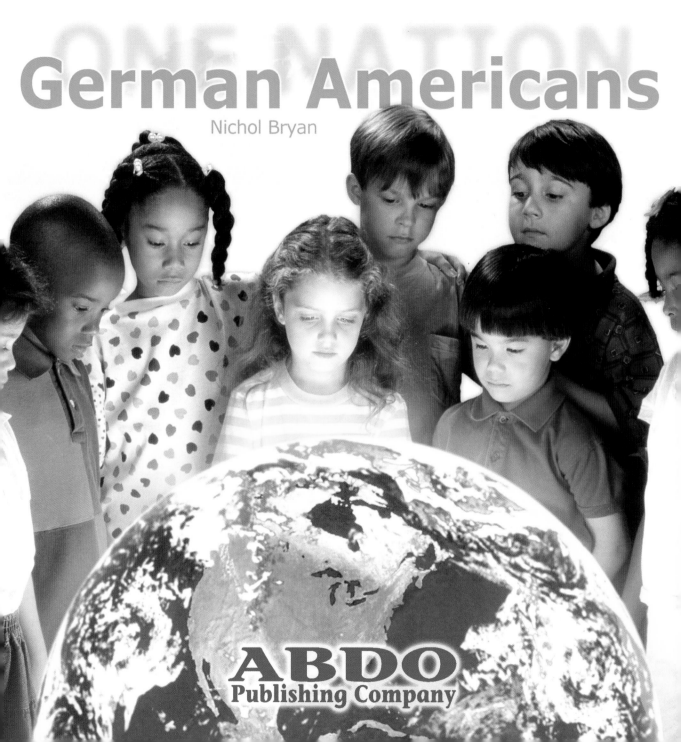

German Americans

ONE NATION

Nichol Bryan

ABDO
Publishing Company

visit us at
www.abdopub.com

Published by ABDO Publishing Company, 4940 Viking Drive, Edina, Minnesota 55435.

Printed in the United States.

Cover Photo: Corbis
Interior Photos: Corbis pp. 1, 2-3, 6, 8, 9, 10, 11, 12, 17, 19, 22, 25, 26, 27, 28, 30-31;
      Kayte Deioma pp. 4-5, 15, 18, 21, 23, 24

Editors: Kate A. Conley, Jennifer R. Krueger, Kristin Van Cleaf
Art Direction & Maps: Neil Klinepier

All of the U.S. population statistics in the One Nation series are taken from the 2000 Census.

Library of Congress Cataloging-in-Publication Data

Bryan, Nichol, 1958-
  German Americans / Nichol Bryan.
     p. cm. -- (One nation)
  Includes index.
  Summary: Provides information on the history of Germany and on the customs, language, religion, and experiences of German Americans.
  ISBN 1-57765-981-3
  1. German Americans--Juvenile literature. [1. German Americans. 2. Immigrants.] I. Title.

E184.G3B84 2003
973'.0431--dc21

                                    2002043634

Contents

German Americans

Germany lies in central Europe. Its beautiful plains, hills, and cities take up about the same area as Montana. Germany's **culture** is old, but the country has changed much in its history. It is this history that has led many Germans to **immigrate** to the United States.

German immigration was highest in the 1800s. Germans joined thousands of other immigrants who came to America seeking new opportunities. Some faced **prejudice**, but all struggled to make the United States their new home.

Once settled, German immigrants helped shape America. In fact, some American **customs** are so common and seem so old that their German origins have been forgotten. Today, Germans still immigrate to the United States, but in much smaller numbers than in the past.

Millions of Americans today have some German heritage.

Germany's Past

Why did nearly 8 million Germans come to the United States? At first, many came for their religion. The 1500s were a time of many religious conflicts in Europe. New ideas in Christianity led to the **Reformation**. But, many rulers were against these new ideas. So in the 1600s, Germans of different faiths began leaving for the American colonies.

During much of this period, Germany was a collection of small states ruled by princes. The years after 1815, when the Napoleonic Wars ended, saw much political confusion. In addition, industrialization began, and craftsmen could not compete with factories. These events resulted in a large wave of **emigration** from Germany, which lasted throughout the 1800s.

Immigrants traveled to America on crowded ships.

Average Germans had little land or money. Crop failures around the 1840s meant many went hungry. Eventually, in 1848, people in Germany **rebelled**, calling for a unified central government. But, the revolution failed. As a result, thousands more fled to the United States.

The Journey from Germany to the United States

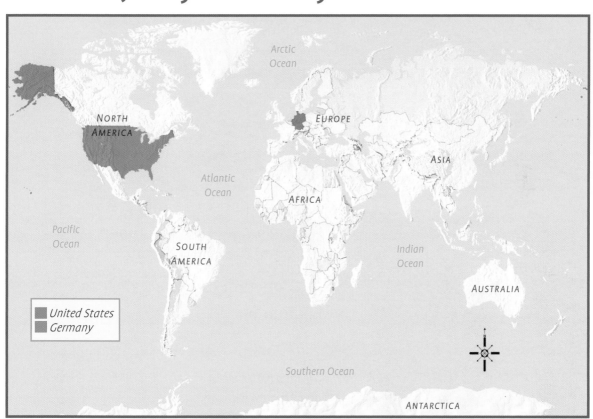

In 1871, the German states were finally united into one empire. In the next few years, Europe faced an **economic depression**, leading to more **emigration**. German entry into the United States was highest in 1882, when 250,600 Germans came to America. But after this time, the economy began to improve, creating more jobs. Though Germans continued to **immigrate** to the United States, by 1900 the rate had slowed.

A German man in the 1920s uses his worthless money as wallpaper.

Between 1914 and 1918, Germany took part in World War I. After Germany lost the war, its economy was in poor shape. Prices were high, German money was worth very little, and there were few jobs. The economy improved briefly but dove again after the U.S. **stock market** crashed in 1929.

Then in 1933, Adolf Hitler came to power. Hitler and his Nazi Party blamed the Jewish people for Germany's problems. They created laws that limited the rights of Jewish people. These acts worried many Germans. Thousands of German Jews fled to the United States and

German immigrants catch their
first glimpse of New York.

Soldiers walk through the ruins of Cologne, Germany.

other countries. Both Jewish and non-Jewish scientists, writers, musicians, scholars, and artists also left the country.

In 1939, Hitler ordered troops to invade Germany's neighbor, Poland. This invasion started World War II. During the war, Hitler ordered Jewish people to be rounded up and kept in **concentration camps**. Hitler and his Nazi government killed 6 million Jewish people in what became known as the Holocaust. The Nazis also killed 4 million non-Jews because the Nazis considered them undesirable for the new society they had planned.

Germany lost the war in 1945, and the country lay in ruins. Thousands of people had lost their homes. Throughout the next 10 years, nearly 375,000 Germans came to the United States. Germans faced other problems, too. The **Allies** had divided Germany and its capital of Berlin in 1945. This led to West Germany becoming a separate country from **communist** East Germany in 1949.

Throughout the next 40 years, the East German **economy** lagged while West Germany grew wealthy. East Germans had few rights, and their own government spied on them. Many people left East Germany for West Germany. The government closed the border in 1952. In 1961, it built the Berlin Wall to keep people from escaping through to West Berlin and West Germany.

In the 1990s, **communism** came to an end all over Europe. The Berlin Wall fell on November 9, 1989. East Germans were finally free to travel. On October 3, 1990, East and West Germany were reunited into one country.

Germany began the task of rebuilding its eastern side. Germans may have sensed new opportunities. Perhaps that is why so many of them stayed in their country in the 1990s. While some Germans still **immigrate** to the United States, they no longer come in large numbers.

The Berlin Wall

In America

In the 1900s and before, most **immigrants** came to the United States by ship. For most, the trip to America was not an easy one. The ships were crowded and diseased. Many passengers were robbed of their possessions. Sadly, many travelers did not survive the voyage.

Once they arrived, Germans built settlements. The first known organized settlement began in 1683. A small group of German families formed Germantown, which is in present-day Pennsylvania. They had chosen the area for its tolerance of different religions. After this, many more Germans belonging to reformed churches immigrated. Because so many were poor, nearly half made the voyage as **redemptioners**.

The Concord Schoolhouse, built in the late 1700s, still stands in the Germantown section of Philadelphia.

These German **immigrants** blended with American society, even fighting in the Revolutionary War. Throughout this time, Germans continued to immigrate to the United States for various reasons. By the last half of the 1800s, millions of Germans had arrived in

German-American Communities

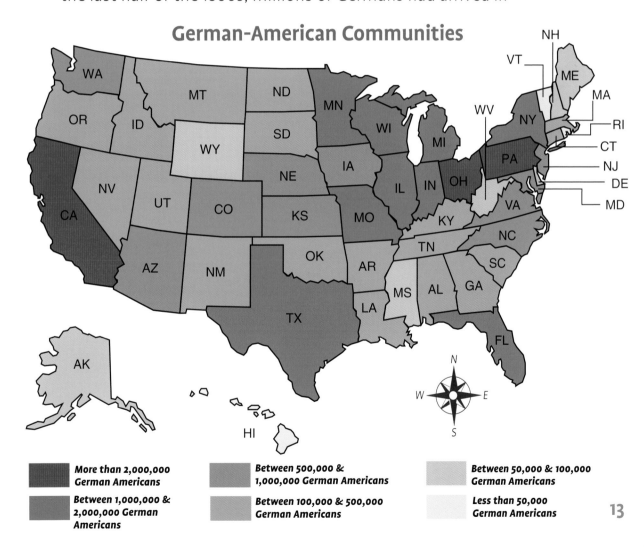

More than 2,000,000 German Americans	**Between 500,000 & 1,000,000 German Americans**	**Between 50,000 & 100,000 German Americans**
Between 1,000,000 & 2,000,000 German Americans	**Between 100,000 & 500,000 German Americans**	**Less than 50,000 German Americans**

America. They worked in factories or became farmers on the Great Plains. By 1900, most people of German **heritage** lived within the "German triangle." Its three points were Cincinnati, Milwaukee, and St. Louis.

Most German Americans were proud of their heritage. Many **customs** continued to be handed down in German communities. When World War I began in 1914, however, many German Americans were torn. They were Americans, but some still had family in Germany.

When the United States joined the war in 1917, many Americans became suspicious of German Americans. High schools stopped offering German as a foreign language. Streets, parks, and even towns were renamed to sound less German. People who wanted sauerkraut on their hot dogs ordered "liberty cabbage" instead. That's because sauerkraut was a German word for a German food!

German Americans felt pressure to stop speaking and reading their native language. As a result, most of America's German-language newspapers stopped publication. German Americans gave up many of their customs to blend into American society. With time, **prejudice** against them lessened.

Like many other people, German Americans were worried when Hitler came to power. A few American clubs held rallies in support of Hitler. Most German Americans, however, spoke out against him and his government. So, when the United States joined World War II, German Americans experienced less **prejudice** than they had during World War I.

Today, German Americans are simply another part of American society. Some places are more German than others. Cities such as Chicago and Milwaukee have large German-American populations. But, German names such as Schmidt, Schneider, and Schwartz can be found in every U.S. telephone book.

A German-American father gives his children basketball tips.

Becoming a Citizen

Germans and other **immigrants** who come to the United States take the same path to citizenship. Immigrants become citizens in a process called naturalization. A government agency called the Immigration and Naturalization Service (INS) oversees this process.

The Path to Citizenship

Applying for Citizenship

The first step in becoming a citizen is filling out a form. It is called the Application for Naturalization. On the application, immigrants provide information about their past. Immigrants send the application to the INS.

Providing Information

Besides the application, immigrants must provide the INS with other items. They may include documents such as marriage licenses or old tax returns. Immigrants must also provide photographs and fingerprints. They are used for identification. The fingerprints are also used to check whether immigrants have committed crimes in the past.

The Interview

Next, an INS officer interviews each immigrant to discuss his or her application and background. In addition, the INS officer tests the immigrant's ability to speak, read, and write in English. The officer also tests the immigrant's knowledge of American civics.

The Oath

Immigrants approved for citizenship must take the Oath of Allegiance. Once immigrants take this oath, they are citizens. During the oath, immigrants promise to renounce loyalty to their native country, to support the U.S. Constitution, and to serve and defend the United States when needed.

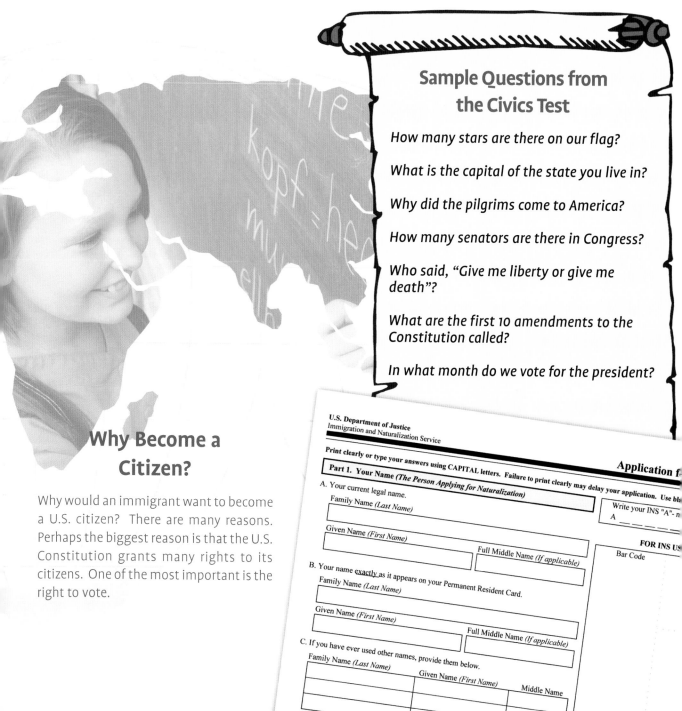

Sample Questions from the Civics Test

How many stars are there on our flag?

What is the capital of the state you live in?

Why did the pilgrims come to America?

How many senators are there in Congress?

Who said, "Give me liberty or give me death"?

What are the first 10 amendments to the Constitution called?

In what month do we vote for the president?

Why Become a Citizen?

Why would an immigrant want to become a U.S. citizen? There are many reasons. Perhaps the biggest reason is that the U.S. Constitution grants many rights to its citizens. One of the most important is the right to vote.

U.S. Department of Justice
Immigration and Naturalization Service

Application f

Print clearly or type your answers using CAPITAL letters. Failure to print clearly may delay your application. Use bla

Part 1. Your Name *(The Person Applying for Naturalization)*

A. Your current legal name.

Family Name *(Last Name)*

Write your INS "A"- n
A _ _ _ _ _ _ _

Given Name *(First Name)*

Full Middle Name *(If applicable)*

FOR INS US

Bar Code

B. Your name exactly as it appears on your Permanent Resident Card.

Family Name *(Last Name)*

Given Name *(First Name)*

Full Middle Name *(If applicable)*

C. If you have ever used other names, provide them below.

Family Name *(Last Name)*

Given Name *(First Name)*

Middle Name

German Ways

German **culture** in the United States is sometimes hard to notice. While many Americans have ties to their German ancestry, many others do not think about their **heritage** on a daily basis. Still, parts of their ancestors' culture are so much a part of the United States that people think of them as simply American.

Family

German Americans have been marrying other **immigrants** for hundreds of years. As a result, more than 57 million Americans have some German heritage. That means almost one of every five U.S. citizens is part German. Are there any Germans in your family tree?

A German-American mother and daughters

Food

Nowhere is German **heritage** more common than at the table. Foods such as hot dogs, bratwurst and other sausages, pastries, dumplings, and potato salad are eaten both in the United States and in Germany. Even pretzels came from Germany, where they are called *Brezeln*. Many of these foods have changed somewhat in America. But, they can still be traced back to their German origins.

A waitress serves traditional German food at a German restaurant in Iowa.

German Traditions

Many German **customs** have been around so long that they seem completely American. For example, many people say *gesundheit* when someone sneezes. They may think it is the same as saying *bless you*. But, this word is actually German and means "health." So when a person says *gesundheit*, he or she is wishing you good health!

Germans have also given Americans a popular holiday tradition, the Christmas tree! Some Americans may think the Christmas tree was an American invention. But, the idea of decorating an evergreen was brought to the United States by German **immigrants**. Some Americans still follow the German practice of first decorating and lighting the tree on Christmas Eve.

Germans have also contributed to education in America. Many German-American immigrant families valued education. They helped build public and private education in the United States. In fact, German immigrants began America's first kindergarten in Wisconsin, in 1855.

Opposite page: Oktoberfest is a festival many German Americans celebrate as part of their heritage.

Celebrations

Though many German celebrations have blended into American **culture**, some still stand out. Oktoberfest, for example, is still celebrated in many communities. In addition, many German Americans take part in German American Day, held on October 6. This day celebrates the history of Germans in the United States and the friendship the country enjoys with Germany today. Both festivals are celebrated with food, folk music, and costumes.

Religion

Many German **immigrants** came to America for religious reasons. In the 1600s and 1700s, many settled in or near present-day Pennsylvania. Many of the immigrants followed a number of Christian faiths. These groups included Lutherans and members of other reform churches, such as Mennonites, Amish, and Moravians.

Many of these immigrants became known as the Pennsylvania Dutch. The word *Dutch* comes from the similar-sounding word *deutsch*, which means "German." They spoke German and developed a dialect called Pennsylvania Dutch. Most of these people now speak English and have become indistinguishable from other Americans.

However, a few groups, such as some Amish, still follow very strict traditional ways. They are mainly farmers who wear simple clothing. They do not

The Pennsylvania Dutch are famous for their artwork.

Amish men in Ohio walk home from a day's work. While the Amish don't use electricity, they do use some modern conveniences.

use electric lights or telephones, and they still drive horse-drawn carts. These habits are based on their religious beliefs.

German Americans today also practice many other religions. Some German Americans are Protestant or Catholic. Others may be Jewish. In fact, many Jewish German Americans have parents or grandparents who fled or are survivors of the Holocaust.

Language

When German **immigrants** first came to America, few knew any English. Their sons and daughters quickly learned English at school. For a time, however, German was spoken in many German-American homes and communities. It was one way that Germans were able to pass on their **culture**.

German-language newspapers were prominent in the United States for hundreds of years. In fact, a newspaper called the *Pennsylvanischer Staatsbote* printed the Declaration of Independence in German just five days after it was signed.

Many of these newspapers lasted until World War I. It was then that many German Americans gave up some of their **customs**, such as speaking German, to show their patriotism. Today, few people in the United States speak German on a daily basis.

German-American children play a game to help them learn German.

A student practices her German skills by naming the parts of a flower.

Talented People

Few **immigrant** groups have contributed more to American **culture** than German Americans. They are leaders in government, science, sports, arts, and entertainment. There are many famous German Americans in every walk of life.

For example, President Dwight D. Eisenhower was of German descent. His family could trace its **heritage** back to Hans N. Eisenhauer, who immigrated to the United States in 1741. Eisenhower was an army general before being elected the thirty-fourth U.S. president in 1952.

Henry Kissinger

Another important German American in the world of politics is former Secretary of State Henry Kissinger. He was born in Fürth, Germany, and **immigrated** to the United States in 1938. Kissinger was the first person born in another country to become secretary of state. He held this post from 1973 to 1977.

German Americans have also been great business successes. German-born Adolphus Busch immigrated to the United States in 1857. He and his father-in-law, Eberhard Anheuser, created the Anheuser-Busch brewery. It is still in business today.

Wernher von Braun

Another successful German-American businessman was Levi Strauss. He left Germany for California in 1850. Strauss offered rugged pants to miners during the California Gold Rush. Today, they are still sold as Levi's jeans.

German-American scientists have ranged from physicist Albert Einstein to space pioneer Wernher von Braun. Einstein developed theories about time and space that had never before been seen. Wernher von Braun helped develop the Saturn V rocket, which took the first astronauts to the moon.

Great German-American writers range from Thomas Mann to Kurt Vonnegut Jr. Thomas Mann was a highly respected German author. He was forced to flee to the United States by the Nazis, and he became a U.S. citizen in 1944. *Doktor Faustus* and *Death in Venice* are two of his best works.

Thomas Mann arrives in New York with his family in 1939.

Kurt Vonnegut Jr. is a descendant of German **immigrants**. He has written many novels showing the dark and funny sides of American life. Vonnegut's novel *Slaughterhouse-Five* is about his experience as a prisoner of war during World War II.

In entertainment, the German-American bandleader Lawrence Welk hosted *The Lawrence Welk Show*. This television program was on the air for more than 15 years, from 1955 to 1971. It was popular all over America for its band music, singers, and dancers. Welk, who grew up in a German community in North Dakota, never lost his slight German accent. Maybe that's because he didn't learn to speak English until he was 21!

In the movies, talented actress Lauren Bacall was the daughter of German immigrants. She acted in many 1940s films. A more recent German-American actress is Sandra Bullock. She was born in Virginia, but her mother is from Germany. Bullock lived in Germany as a child and still speaks some German.

Germany is very much a part of America. Its people and **culture** have helped make the United States what it is today. For many Americans, their German roots are just one part of their distant **heritage**. Others strongly identify with their German background, carrying on many German traditions in the United States.

Glossary

allies - people or countries that agree to help each other in times of need. During World War II, Great Britain, France, the United States, and the Soviet Union were called the Allies.

communism - a social and economic system in which everything is owned by the government and is distributed to the people as needed.

concentration camp - a camp where political enemies and prisoners of war are held.

culture - the customs, arts, and tools of a nation or people at a certain time.

customs - the habits of a group that are passed on through generations.

depression - a period of economic trouble when there is little buying or selling and many people are out of work.

economy - the way a nation uses its money, goods, and natural resources.

emigration - to leave one's country and move to another. People who emigrate are called emigrants.

heritage - the handing down of something from one generation to the next.

immigration - entry into another country to live. People who immigrate are called immigrants.

prejudice - hatred of a particular group based on factors such as race or religion.

rebel - to disobey an authority or the government.

redemptioners - poor Europeans who allowed the ship's captain to sell them when they arrived in America. Redemptioners worked until their purchase price was paid.

Reformation - a religious movement in the sixteenth century. Some people worked to change the Catholic Church. Other people formed Protestant churches.

stock market - a place where stocks and bonds, which represent parts of businesses, are bought and sold.

Saying It

Adolphus Busch - uh-DAWL-fuhs BUSH
Brezeln - BRAY-tsuhln
deutsch - DOYTSH
Eberhard Anheuser - A-buhr-hahrt AHN-hoy-sehr
Fürth - FOORT
gesundheit - guh-ZYUNT-hite
Henry Kissinger - HEHN-ree KIH-suhn-juhr
Kurt Vonnegut - KURT VAH-nih-guht
Levi Strauss - LEE-vi STROUWS
Pennsylvanischer Staatsbote - pen-suhl-FAH-nihsh-ehr shtats-BOH-tuh
Thomas Mann - TOH-mahs MAHN
Wernher von Braun - VUHR-nuhr fawn-BROWN

Web Sites

To learn more about German Americans, visit ABDO Publishing Company on the World Wide Web at **www.abdopub.com**. Web sites about German Americans are featured on our Book Links page. These links are routinely monitored and updated to provide the most current information available.

Index